JAZZ

by Walter Dean Myers

illustrated by Christopher Myers

Holiday House / New York

With thanks to Daniel Burwasser, PhD,
for his help with music terminology, history,
and theory.

Text copyright © 2006 by Walter Dean Myers
Illustrations copyright © 2006 by Christopher Myers
All Rights Reserved | Printed and bound in July 2018 at
TWP Sdn Bhd, Johor Bahru, Johor, Malaysia

The artist created the illustrations by painting black ink on
acetate and placing it over acrylic.

The fonts are Clarendon Rough and Pablo.

www.holidayhouse.com

9 10

LIBRARY OF CONGRESS CATALOGING-IN-PUBLICATION DATA
Myers, Walter Dean, 1937–2014
Jazz / by Walter Dean Myers ;
illustrated by Christopher Myers.— 1st ed.
p. cm.
Summary: Illustrations and rhyming text
celebrate the roots of jazz music.
ISBN–13: 978–0–8234–1545–8
ISBN–10: 0–8234–1545–7 (hardcover)
[1. Jazz–Fiction. 2. Musicians–Fiction. 3. Stories in rhyme.]
I. Myers, Christopher, ill. II. Title.
PZ8.3.M9954 Jaz 2006
[E]–dc22 2005052639

ISBN–13: 978–0–8234–2173–2 (paperback)

Design: Yvette Lenhart

JAZZ

To the children
of New Orleans

W. D. M.
& C. M.

INTRODUCTION

When we use the term *jazz*, we are talking about an approach to music that is exciting and creative—one that relies on improvisation and spontaneity. American in its origins, today jazz is played throughout the world in performances that celebrate both the history of this rich music as well as its immediacy. There are many kinds of jazz—swing, be-bop, cool jazz, fusion, and free jazz are just a few—but its fundamental premise remains the same: musicians "composing" something new as they perform.

The jazz musician might begin with a well-known melody and then interpret it according to his or her own personality and musical training. In every instance, improvisation is a key element of jazz.

The second major element of jazz is rhythm. Early jazz often served as dance music, but even as the music and performances grew increasingly complex and abstract, its strong rhythm continued to pull in the listener.

A blending of two musical traditions, African and European, contributed to the development of jazz. African music, with its five-tone, or pentatonic, scales and complex rhythms, came to North America during the slave trade. In 1834 James R. Creecy described a black gathering in Congo Square in New Orleans:

"Groups of fifties and hundreds may be seen in different sections of the square, with banjos, tom-toms, violins, jawbones, triangles, and various other instruments from which harsh or dulcet sounds may be extracted . . ."

By the end of the Civil War, there were many skilled black musicians, and black popular music quickly began dividing into several distinct styles. Gospel and spiritual music grew out of the black church. The blues flourished throughout the Deep South in informal clubs and parties. Early black musicians from the slave states, who had been forbidden to learn to read and write, usually played their instruments by "ear"—that is, they learned tunes and chords by listening and imitating others. What they heard, however, was not only African-influenced music, but the European music being played by white musicians.

At the same time, white musicians heard black music and borrowed freely from it, using black harmonics and sometimes black scales. Black musicians did the same with European music, and soon popular music began to show a melding of these different traditions. The use of the African, or "blues," scale and African rhythms changed the feel of European music and made it "swing." The dance halls and small clubs in which most black musicians played allowed them more freedom and experimentation than they could have had in formal concert halls. Since so many black musicians were still not formally trained in reading musical notation, there had to be some way of knowing what the other players were going to do so that they could perform together.

To solve this problem, these musicians began using European chord structures as the basis of their music. By understanding which chords would be played and in what order, musicians could stay within the same harmonic structure. A player could stray from the melody as originally composed and still make music that sounded as if it belonged to the same composition if he or she were playing within the same chord structure as the others. Learning chord structures made American popular music, which was written and played in the European style, readily available to be played by these emerging artists. It also encouraged improvisation, because the players realized that the variations within the chord structures were often the most interesting parts of the song or composition. Black musicians, still outside of the mainstream in American popular music as America entered the age of technology, took the lead in musical improvisation.

Somewhere around 1910 this hot new music was described by a new term—*jazz*. There are conflicting versions of what the word meant and why it was used, but by the outbreak of the First World War, the word was used throughout the country.

World War I saw black Americans going to Europe for the first time in large numbers. The segregated black military outfits had their own bands and introduced Europeans to jazz. James Reese Europe took an outstanding group of musicians through France as the head of the 369th Infantry Band, the army's most famous musical ensemble. This coincided with another major influence, the growth of the recording industry.

Records spread jazz throughout the world. To Europeans it represented the freedom found in American performance styles. To American musicians it represented a challenging new way of approaching music. By the mid twenties there were bands calling themselves jazz orchestras all over the United States, and the era itself was christened the "jazz age." All musicians, black and white, understood the principles of swing and improvisation.

Not all jazz will be loved by all people, but anyone who understands the history and development of the art, and the dedication and genius of the true jazz performance, can appreciate its beauty and depth.

Today, different artists reinterpret the music according to their own sensibilities, and new listeners bring their own tastes and understanding to the music. Ultimately it becomes, like all art, a dialogue between the artist and the audience, a dialogue that is still vital, still fun, and still America's gift to the world.

W. D. M.

JAZZ

Start with *rhythm*
Start with *the heart*
Drumming *in tongues*
Along the Nile
A black man's drum
Speaks
LOVE
Start with
RHYTHM
Start with
the HEART
Work songs
Gospel
Triumph
Despair
Voices
Lifted
From *the soul*

LOUIE, LOUIE, HOW YOU PLAY SO SWEET?

Louie, Louie, how you play so sweet?
What have you heard, down on Bourbon Street?

"I heard London

Turned it black and blue

Heard Copenhagen

Played it my way, too

Heard a sad song

Swung it into joy

Heard a bad tune

Spanked it like a naughty boy."

Louie, Louie, how you play so sweet?
What have you heard, down on Bourbon Street?

AMERICA'S MUSIC

What did the world see?

What did the world hear?

Black men sweating in 4/4 time

Behind the beat, around the beat

Bending the in-between

Strings crying like midnight widows

Horns tearing down Jericho walls

A clarinet sassing

Its way through

a Sunday-night sermon

And the chorus calling out blues!
And ragtime!
And jazz!

From Mississippi to Harlem

While the folks across the ocean

were just saying

AMERICA

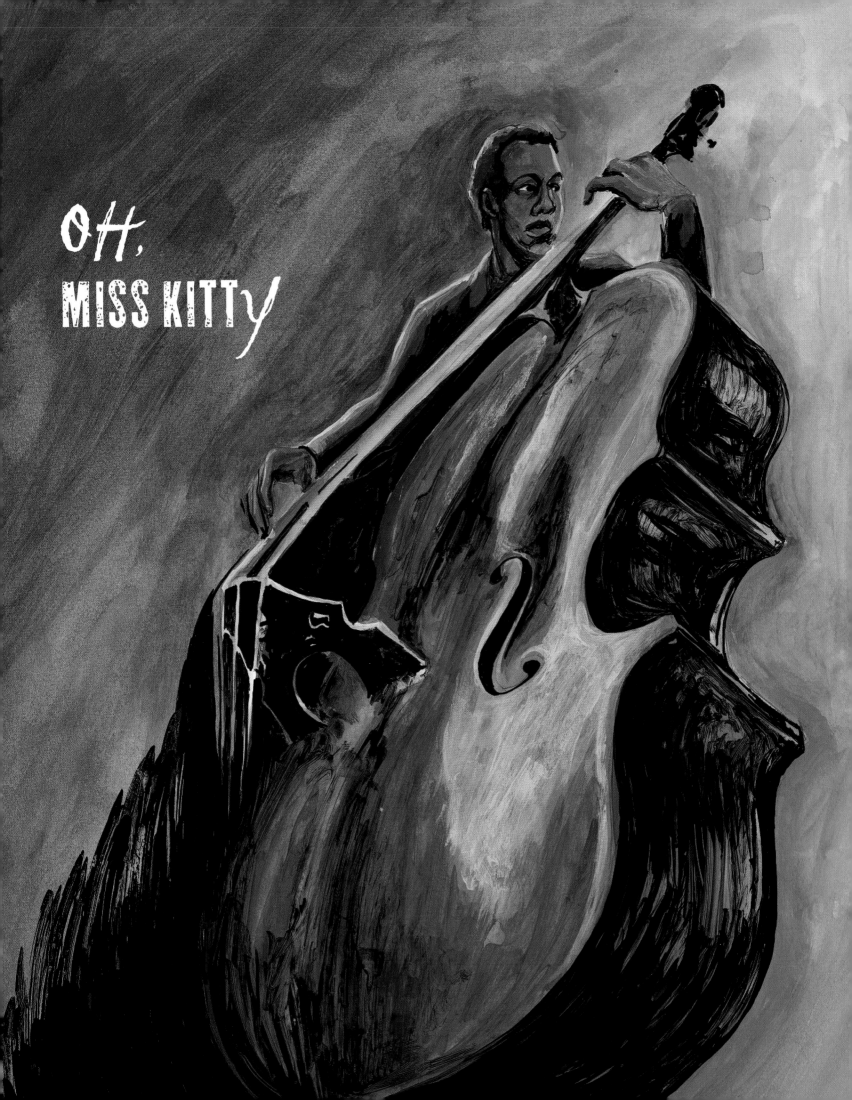

Oh, Miss Kitty,

she's as round as she is tall

I said Oh, Miss Kitty,

she's as round as she is tall

Ain't nothing about Miss Kitty

you would say is small

Dance, Miss Kitty

Dance till the break of dawn

You been dancing, Miss Kitty

Since the day that you were born

Oh, Miss Kitty,

she's in love with the piano man

"Tickle them ivories, boy!"

Oh, Miss Kitty,

she's in love with the piano man

"Hit the white keys, too."

He's a slitty-eyed gangster

but plays like he got a plan

Dance, Miss Kitty

Dance till the break of dawn

You been dancing, Miss Kitty

Since the day that you were born

"What that saxophone man doing?"

He plays it high

and he plays with so much feeling

Yeah, he plays it high

and he plays with so much feeling

Go get some water

'cause he's burning up the ceiling

DANCE, Miss Kitty

Dance till the break of dawn

You been dancing, Miss Kitty

Since the day that you were born

STRIDE

We got jiving in our bones, and it won't leave us alone—we're really moving

jiving *bones*

We got pride in our stride, and we know it's all the style—we're steady grooving

pride *stride*

This piano's hard and driving, and the tones are getting to me—hear them talking

driving *tones*

There's a glide to the ride, and the feeling's coming through me—the bass is walking

glide *ride*

I hear singing in my heart, yes, it's rhythm, yes, it's art, no use in stalling

singing *heart*

I got jump in my feet, and I'm turning up the heat, left hand hauling

jump *feet*

I'm out here swinging from the start, can't get no higher

swinging *start*

We got bump in the beat where the crazy rhythms meet. This band's on fire!

BUMP *BEAT*

GOOD-BYE TO OLD BOB JOHNSON

Well, good-bye to old Bob Johnson

We'll haul his body slow

There's a white horse a-striding

A sad deacon riding

Six men to lay him low

The drums are solemn as we walk along

The banjo twangs a gospel song

Let the deacons preach and the widow cry

While a sad horn sounds a last good-bye

Good-bye to old Bob Johnson

Good-bye

(*Faster*)

Move along, move along, Bob Johnson

I know you're striding high

Yes, the church band is *swinging*

And the sisters are *singing*

A jazzy lullaby

We told Saint Peter

that you're on your way

You brought your horn

and you're here to stay

We're stepping

and we're hipping

and we're dipping, too

We're celebrating,

syncopating,

and it's all for you

The trumpets blow some hot licks,

and they start to climb

Along the road to heaven

in 4/4 time

Every face is smiling

and every eye is dry

Good-bye, Bob Johnson, *good-bye*

TWENTY-FINGER JACK

Well, the walls are shaking,

and the ceiling's coming down

'Cause twenty-finger Jack

has just come back to town

The keyboard's jumping,

and the music's going round

and round

If he had any sense,

he left it in the lost-and-found

Here he go

Be ba boodie, be ba boodie, boo
Be ba boodie, be ba ba ba, boodie, boo

There's a steady beat walking,

and the melody's talking, too

If you ain't moving,

there must be something wrong with you

My knees don't like it,

but my feet just got to dance

My heels can't follow,

but my toes will take a chance

Be ba boodie, be ba boodie, boo
Be ba boodie, be ba ba ba, boodie, boo

Drop your blues,

and throw away that frown

'Cause twenty-finger Jack

has just come back to town

BE-BOP

Oh be-bop be-bop, oh whee,

OH WHEEE!

Oh be-bop be-bop,

don't you dig I'm free?

Oh be-bop be-bop,

do you dig my jive?

This jazz that I'm playing

is keeping me alive!

The sweet honey changing

And the mood rearranging

And the ax that I'm grinding

And the melody I'm finding

Goes screa—min',
goes screamin,
goes screa—screa-screamin

To the moon!

Oh bippety-bop bop, oh wheee!

OH WHEE!

A bippety-bop square

can't mess with me!

A bippety-bop snake

can't bite my style

But a bippety-bop chick

can stay awhile

'Cause the jazz that we're playing

And the licks that we're laying

And the dues that we're paying

And the blues that we're slaying

Go screa—min', go screamin',
go screa—screa-screamin

To the moon!

OH YEAH

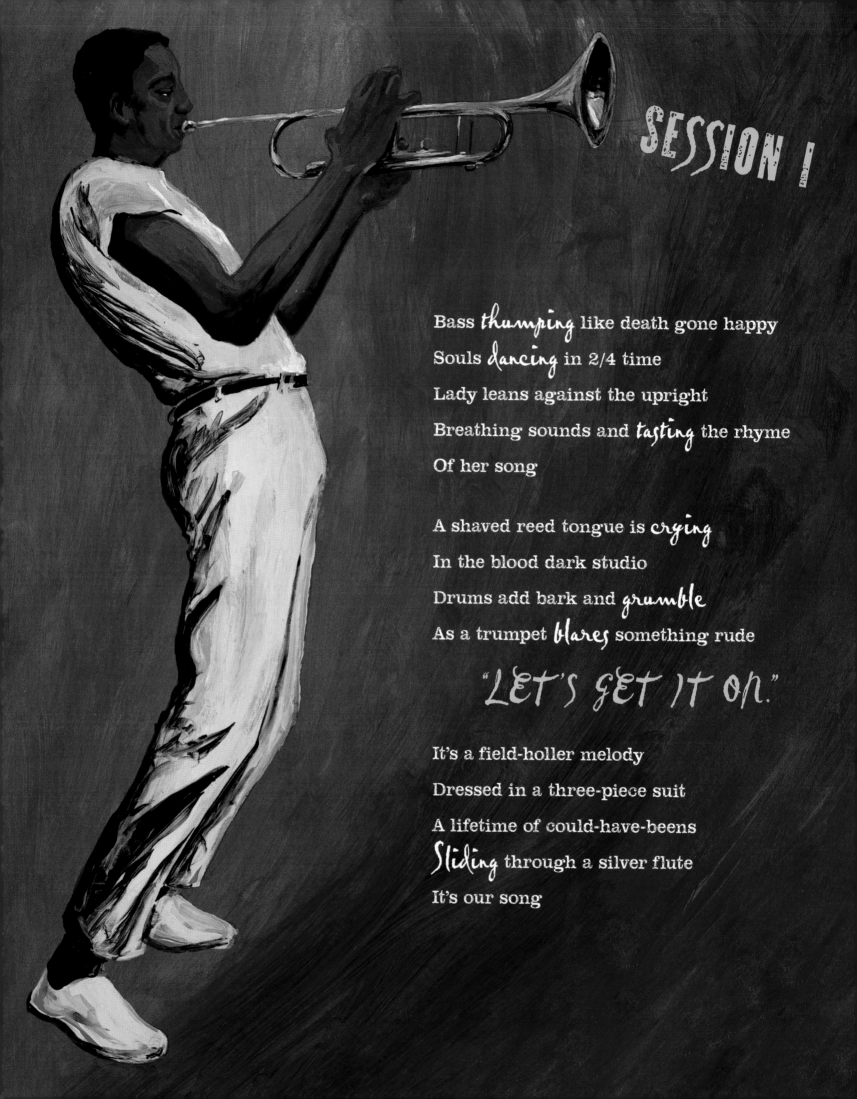

Bass *thumping* like death gone happy
Souls *dancing* in 2/4 time
Lady leans against the upright
Breathing sounds and *tasting* the rhyme
Of her song

A shaved reed tongue is *crying*
In the blood dark studio
Drums add bark and *grumble*
As a trumpet *blares* something rude
"LET'S GET IT ON."

It's a field-holler melody
Dressed in a three-piece suit
A lifetime of could-have-beens
Sliding through a silver flute
It's our song

A sultry love song, sassy as a summer day,

goes dancing from my heart and fills my mind

with such sweet things to say,

Like I love you oh so much

and I tremble when you touch my hand.

Can you understand?

Or can't you really see

what your beauty does to me

and your every word to me is my command?

It's our song. Our love song.

Can you hear it just beginning

or am I just imagining those precious sounds?

It's a warm night, and much to my delight

my heart beats like a cool jazz bass,

making a special place for us to follow

as we walk on the edges of a dream

or is that horn man painting the edges of a love moonbeam?

Are those chords the heart of reason

or is this just the silly season to fall in love?

The melody and beat are blending

to a happy-ever ending for you and me.

It's a love song. A sultry love song. All right.

JAZZ VOCAL

BLUE CREEPS IN

Blue peeps in

Blue sits on my windowsill

Waiting for me to come out

To swing out onto the empty avenue

And go walking through the

Rainy streets the way we used

To do

Blue puts her arms

Around me

Blue starts into

Astound me

With her witty repartee

Blue walks a little bit

Ahead and turns to

See me and her smile

Reminds me of

You, too

We wander through

The summer rain

And don't mind getting

Slightly damp

Because we're

So much in love

That nothing matters

In this whole world

But the moment and

The fact

That we're together

No matter what the weather

It's all laughter and no

Boo-hoo

Then it's time for me

To go home

And in that direction

I start to roam

Down familiar streets

I nod at the neon

Lights and they

Wink back in sweet affection

The wet streets

Shimmer good night

The raindrops hiss

Their sorry sighs 'cause

They know just

How very much

I'm missing you

SESSION II

Mercy, mercy, mercy
Please have mercy, Mr. Slide Trombone
Mercy, mercy, mercy
Please have mercy, Mr. Slide Trombone
My baby's gone and left me
I got to play till midnight
Then go home all alone

The piano man is tinkling
Tinkling all up and down the keys
The drummer man is working
His rhythm got me on my knees
I'm playing E-flat minor on my saxophone
But I still know I got to go home all alone

So have mercy, mercy, mercy
Have mercy, Mr. Slide Trombone
But mercy, mercy, mercy
Have mercy, Mr. Slide Trombone
HAVE MERCY, Mr. Slide Trombone

NOW I COME In

There's crazy rhythm in the drums

You can feel it when it comes

It's SO cool

You can hear the bass man

Humming

As his fingers start to

Strumming

He's steady stroking in a

Music pool

The piano's come alive and

I know that she'll be driving

Through the night

And it's SO right

You know. . . You know

And now I come in

This horn is my heart

And I've got to play my part

That takes you to another place

And time

This melody from memory

Makes harmonies that reach to be

So much more than a simple tune

Or rhyme

I'll take you as far as I can go

I'll blow as hard as I can blow

I'll reach for the stars

Blow notes around Mars

And then you come in

AND
THEN
YOU
COME
In

THREE VOICES

Bass:

Thum, thum, thum, and
thumming
I feel the ocean rhythm
coming
Thum, thum, thum, and
thumming
I feel the midnight passion
humming

Piano:

Sweet and gentle, so surprising

Music fills us, hear it rising

Like a charming angel choir

Reaching, preaching souls on fire

Horn:

What can I add with my horn?

Is it a new sound born because we are

Together?

Or is it just a melody that's leading me

To where I want to be and loosed from

My tether?

And is it really not surprising that our

Spirits are all rising and drawing us

Even higher

Three souls on fire

Um-hmmm

I hear the call of the cornet
I hear a swinging clarinet
They're playing HOT jazz in the heat
Of old New Orleans
The rattling banjo pays its dues
To the Preservation blues
They're playing HOT jazz in the heat
Of old New Orleans
There's a crazy syncopation
And it's tearing through the nation
And it's bringing sweet elation
To every single tune
It's jazz
There's a drummer rat-a-tatting
There's a patent shoe that's patting
While a laid-back cat is scatting
About flying to the moon
It's jazz
In the HEAT of New Orleans

GLOSSARY OF
JAZZ TERMS

Ax: A slang term for any musical instrument

Ballad: A slow tune

Be-bop: In the 1940s, some young jazz musicians developed a style that challenged the slower and smoother jazz common to the period. This new style was very complex, considerably less melodic, and technically extremely difficult. Its jumps from low to high notes (think a low *Be* jumping to a high *Bop!*) gave the style its name.

Blow: A slang term meaning to play an instrument, even a piano

Blues: A forerunner to jazz that uses a modified five-tone African scale. Most jazz is blues influenced.

Boogie: A blues piano style using a strong and steady left-hand pattern that is repeated while the right hand plays an improvised melody. Sometimes called boogie-woogie.

Changes: Jazz is a melody played over a progression of chords. The chord patterns are either memorized or prearranged so that the player knows what chord to move, or "change," to.

Chops: Technical ability. "Man, his breath is bad, but he's got some good chops!"

Chord: Three or more notes played at the same time; provides the basic harmony at any given moment

Cool Jazz: In the 1950s, some jazz musicians rebelled against the fast pace of be-bop and became "cool," which is a more relaxed sounding form of jazz.

Free Jazz: From its beginnings through the 1950s, jazz consisted of melody lines over an underlying chord structure. Free jazz carried improvisation a step further, liberating the musician from the chord structure.

Fusion: The combining of jazz techniques with other kinds of music, such as rock in the 1970s. This concept upset many jazz purists and blurred the distinctions between types of music.

Hard Bop: As cool jazz was a reaction to be-bop, hard bop was a reaction to cool jazz. It uses a stronger rhythmical base, with heavy urban blues overtones.

Hip: The state of being "in the know." "Man, he said life is hard when you ain't got no money, but I was already hip to that!"

Improvisation: The spontaneous creation of new melodies or harmonies during a performance. This can include improvising over a chord structure, changing a tune, or creating an entirely new piece.

Jazz: A style of playing dependent on syncopated rhythms, improvisation, and freedom of expression. The word itself most likely comes from the French Creole word *jass*, which finds its root in the French *chasse*, meaning to hunt, chase, or speed up.

Latin Jazz: A blend of jazz and South American, Puerto Rican, or Cuban music, often using repeated bass figures

Mainstream: A loose term that generally refers to traditional jazz

Melody: The top line in a composition; the tune

Modern Jazz: Jazz created since 1945

Pentatonic Scale: The five-tone scale found in many parts of the world, which was brought to America from Africa. This scale gives jazz much of its bluesy feeling.

Ragtime: A complex music, distinguished by strong syncopation, that extended the range of European popular music rhythmically and was one of the many bridges to jazz

Riff: A repeated phrase, usually rather short

Stride Piano: A piano style popular in the 1920s and 1930s in which the left hand sets up a rhythm by "striding" between the lowest notes on the piano and the middle notes, while the right hand plays either a melody line or runs

Swing: In jazz, a shifting in rhythm that seems to propel the tune by shortening the second beat in any two-beat configuration while delaying the accent so that the listener mentally moves to the next bar. The resulting feeling is that of "swing." Often refers to the sound of the big jazz bands.

JAZZ TIME LINE

Early jazz was frowned on in much of America.
Ministers spoke out against it, many bands refused
to play it, and record companies ignored it. The
history of the genre is often re-created by informal
interviews, sketchy newspaper accounts, and folklore.
Nevertheless, here are a few interesting dates:

1800s .... Congo Square in New Orleans is the only place in America where African music and dance are legally allowed and encouraged. Elsewhere, both the music and the dancing are considered "savage" and "uncivilized."

1865 .... The Civil War ends. Black music has already been noted and mimicked by white composers such as Stephen Foster. Black musicians gain access to professionally made instruments.

1893 .... William C. Handy, age twenty, leads a band at the World's Columbian Exposition, the world's fair, in Chicago, thus exposing a white northern audience to black musicians.

1899 .... Scott Joplin's "Maple Leaf Rag" is published. It will sell more than one hundred thousand copies.

1900s .... A combination of ragtime and blues is heard in New Orleans.

1913 .... Louis Armstrong plays in the Colored Waif's Home for Boys band.

1915 .... King Oliver forms the first version of his Creole Jazz Band in New Orleans.

1918 .... James Reese Europe, as a lieutenant in World War I, wows Europe with his all-black band of virtuoso musicians.

1921 .... Jazz performances are banned in Zion, Illinois.

1922 .... The record industry discovers black America. Kid Ory, in California, and Fats Waller, in New York, begin to make recordings.

1923 .... King Oliver's band records "Just Gone" and "Canal Street Blues" with twenty-two-year-old Louis Armstrong.

1925 .... In a year in which pianist James P. Johnson records in New York and Louis Armstrong records with his group, the Hot Five, the Ku Klux Klan marches in

1932 .... Duke Ellington records "It Don't Mean A Thing (If It Ain't Got That Swing)."

1935 .... Billie Holiday records with Teddy Wilson. George Gershwin opens his jazz-inspired opera, *Porgy and Bess*, in New York to mixed reviews.

1938 .... Band leader Benny Goodman performs with his integrated group at Carnegie Hall. King Oliver, living in poverty, dies in Georgia.

1941 .... "Take the 'A' Train," by the great composer Billy Strayhorn, is recorded by Duke Ellington. Be-bop is invented by Dizzy Gillespie, Charlie Parker, Bud Powell, and others.

1945 .... Miles Davis leaves Juilliard to play with Charlie Parker.

1956 .... The cool jazz movement, led by white musicians, flourishes on the West Coast. It widens the audience for jazz.

1960 .... Miles Davis releases *Sketches of Spain* using classical Spanish music.

1966 .... Duke Ellington receives the President's Gold Medal on behalf of President Lyndon B. Johnson for his contributions to American art.

1978 .... President Jimmy Carter hosts a jazz concert at the White House, acknowledging the contribution of the music to America.

1987 .... Wynton Marsalis cofounds Jazz at Lincoln Center for the Performing Arts.

1997 .... Wynton Marsalis is the first jazz musician to win the Pulitzer Prize for Music.

TODAY ... Jazz is played throughout the world, in concert halls, night clubs, and theaters.